Young Explorers

AROUND
ROME

Text by Daniela Celli

Illustrations by Laura Re

A NOTE FOR PARENTS

"Quanto sei bella Roma" (How beautiful you are, Rome). These are the lyrics from a popular Italian song from the 1930s, and while no one would disagree with this sentiment, you may feel overwhelmed at the mere thought of exploring the Italian capital with children. Where do you start in a city that has over nine hundred churches, dozens of museums, and even an entire country within it?
The answer's simple: let your children choose where they want to take you, with the help of this guide and the stories it tells.
It doesn't contain everything that the Eternal City has to offer, as visiting (or describing, for that matter) it all would be impossible!

HOWEVER, YOU WILL FIND FOUR FUN ITINERARIES FOR CHILDREN, FULL OF LEGENDS AND FUN FACTS, DESIGNED TO HELP KIDS LEARN ABOUT A METROPOLIS WHERE EVEN THE STREET NUMBERS HAVE A STORY TO TELL.

You can use this book to play-travel at home - and to really travel, of course!
I've included all the things that my own kids loved when they were little, which I hope will enchant you as much as they do your little explorers.

To my parents (all four of them!), who showed me the beauty of the world, and gave me the freedom to explore it.

Daniela Celli

HI FRIENDS, LET ME INTRODUCE MYSELF

Good morning, little explorers!
My name's Lupetta, which means "little she-wolf," and my family has lived in Rome for
as long as we can remember! I'm so excited to show you around my beautiful city.
Every single stone in Rome has a fascinating, mysterious, or curious story to tell,
so I assure you we won't ever get bored!
Did you know, for example, that a cannon is fired on the Janiculum Hill every
day at noon? Or that there's a bizarre lie detector in the Ripa neighborhood?
If you're curious to know more, then let's get going!
We'll explore thanks to four fun itineraries, which will take us up and down
the streets of the Italian capital, exploring hills, squares, palazzos, and ancient ruins.
We'll even be taking a trip abroad!
Each itinerary starts with a map, which shows all the places we'll be visiting.
If you get thirsty, we can stop at one of the many *nasoni* (drinking fountains),
and if you get hungry (I'm always hungry!), well, Rome is full of delicious things to eat.
Finally, between one wonder and another,
we'll have time to play a few games.
And don't forget to keep your eyes open!

ARE YOU READY?
LET'S GO!

CONTENTS

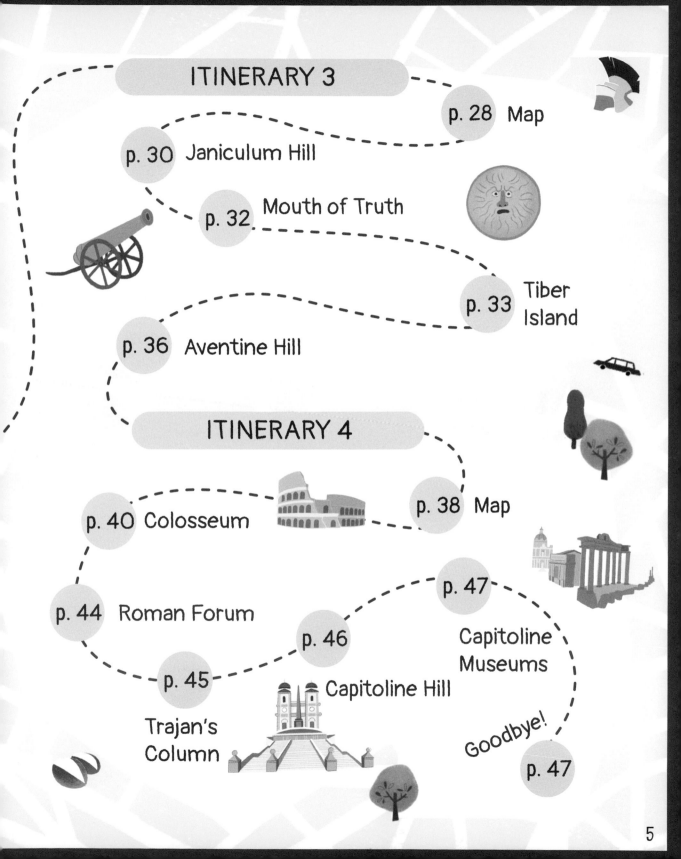

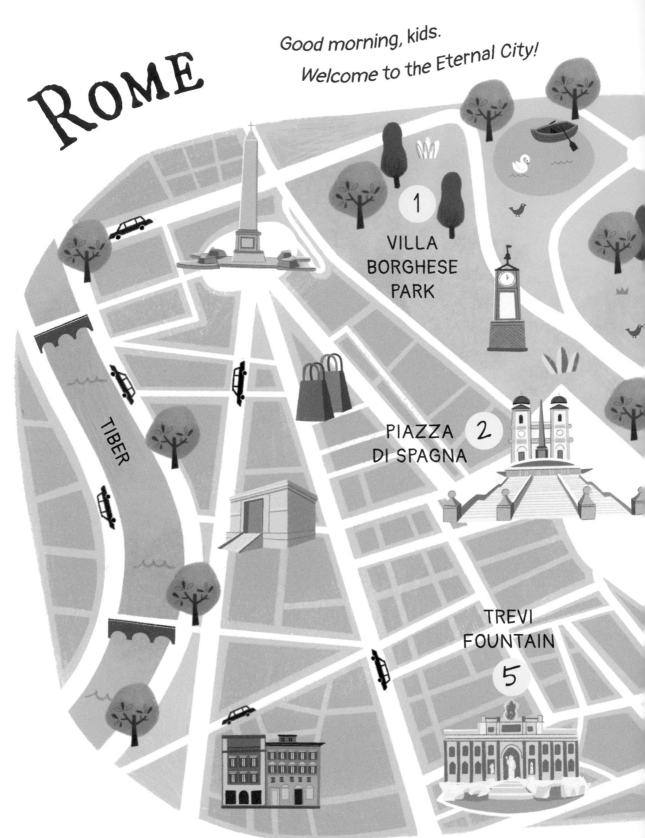

ROME

Good morning, kids.
Welcome to the Eternal City!

1 VILLA BORGHESE PARK

TIBER

PIAZZA DI SPAGNA 2

TREVI FOUNTAIN 5

Our first day in Rome will start with a visit to a wonderful park in the middle of the city. After taking a fun boat ride, and seeing a "half-sunken ship," we'll go on a monster hunt, then head down into a mysterious underground tunnel covered in skeletons, and finally stop in Piazza di Trevi, where an important mission awaits us.

PALAZZETTO ZUCCARI

3

4

CAPUCHIN CRYPT

• A City Within the City

Rome's old city center is divided into *22 districts*: the first is *Monti*, a neighborhood which spreads over three hills, and the last is *Prati*, whose symbol is CASTEL SANT'ANGELO. Keep your eyes open as we walk around the city: each neighborhood is indicated by a plaque bearing a NUMBER, its name, and a coat of arms that tells a story about a small part of the city.

• An Ancient Nickname

The first person to call Rome the ETERNAL CITY was a Latin poet who lived more than two thousand years ago.

IT WAS SUCH A PERFECT NICKNAME THAT IT HAS BEEN USED EVER SINCE!

VILLA BORGHESE

Should we start exploring the city
from one of its amazing green spaces?

Villa Borghese is one of the largest urban parks in Europe! It's an OASIS in the heart of the city, where you can skate, cycle, or have a picnic, or even admire the artwork in the *Borghese Gallery*, pretend you're a sailor, watch a PUPPET show at the San Carlino theater, or see a movie in the world's smallest theater!

• (Almost) All Aboard!

Villa Borghese's beautiful lake is in the center of the park. You can rent a rowboat, then navigate your way around the islet that houses the temple of Asclepius, the God of Medicine. Just steer clear of the ducks and swans as you go!

• A Water Clock

Just a stone's throw from the *panoramic terrace on the Pincian hill*, there's an INGENIOUS INVENTION that was made by a Dominican friar in 1867.

The pendulum of this unusual clock moves thanks to water, which falls from above and fills two basins.

CLEVER, ISN'T IT?

WHY DON'T YOU GO PLAY ON THE LAKE, WHILE I, UM... I'LL WAIT FOR YOU ON LAND: THIS LITTLE WOLF ISN'T CRAZY ABOUT WATER!

Can you find all the animals in the pond?

Seek and Find

- 3 turtles
- 2 toads
- 2 fish
- 5 ducks
- 2 swans.

PIAZZA DI SPAGNA

From above, this square looks like a large butterfly with triangle-shaped wings!

Piazza di Spagna is one of the most famous squares in Rome. This elegant outdoor "living room" is surrounded by beautiful buildings, and is home to the Spanish Steps, an amazing STAIRCASE that has connected the square with the *Church of Trinità dei Monti* for three centuries. There used to be a steep cliff where the 135 travertine steps are today.
SHALL WE CLIMB TO THE TOP?

• The Sinking Barcaccia

In the center of the square, there's a magnificent *fountain* in the shape of a boat, or rather a BARCACCIA, a sort of boat used for transporting goods down the *Tiber*. LOOK AT IT CAREFULLY: does it look like it's sinking to you? Well, it is! It seems that the sculptor PIETRO BERNINI was inspired by a boat that was carried into the square during a flood.

PALAZZETTO ZUCCARI

Shall we go on a monster hunt?

Built by FEDERICO ZUCCARI in 1590, this imaginative building is nicknamed the *House of Monsters*, because of the terrifying decorations on the door and window frames. They look like giant open mouths!

DO THEY FRIGHTEN YOU? If the answer's NO, turn the book round: you're ready for the next place on our tour!
IF THEY DO, GO DIRECTLY
TO PAGE 12.

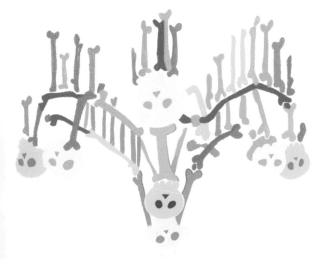

THE CAPUCHIN CRYPT

Follow me, my intrepid friends!

A few minutes from *Piazza di Spagna*, there's one of the most disturbing and mysterious places in Rome. Inside the *Church of Santa Maria dell'Immacolata*, there's a CRYPT decorated with the bones of thousands of friars!
A mysterious artist used skulls, tibias, vertebrae, and entire skeletons to create chandeliers, columns, arches, and ornaments to line the ceiling and walls.

THE TREVI FOUNTAIN

This is the biggest fountain in Rome!

Did you know there's a Roman legend about this old fountain? That's right! If you close your eyes and toss a COIN over your shoulder into the water, you will definitely return to Rome one day!

BUT BE CAREFUL, FOR IT TO WORK, YOU HAVE TO TURN AROUND IN TIME TO SEE THE COIN FALL INTO THE WATER!

• The Lovers' Fountain

On the right-hand side of the monument, there's a simple stone drinking fountain where two jets of water cross each other, probably to help Roman women fill their buckets faster. Legend has it that couples who drink from this fountain, and then break the glass they used, will stay in love forever.

• What Happens to the Coins?

Municipal employees collect the coins, after which they're cleaned, dried, and donated to charity. More than one million euros are raised every year!

Are you ready for another adventure?

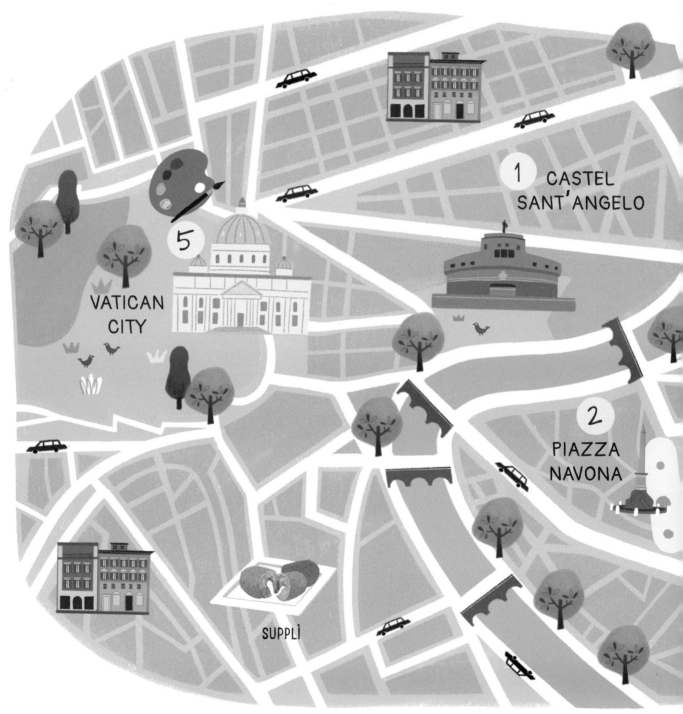

5 VATICAN CITY

1 CASTEL SANT'ANGELO

2 PIAZZA NAVONA

SUPPLÌ

ITINERARY 2

An exciting journey awaits us today! We'll start by visiting a beautiful CASTLE, where we'll hear about a legend and see a SECRET PASSAGE no less. We'll explore a SQUARE that was once a stadium, as well as a lake, and then we'll discover the MYSTERIES of one of the greatest buildings in the ancient world.

We'll visit a church with a MAGICAL ROOF, go hunting for a certain FELINE and, for our last stop, I'll be taking you...abroad.

ARE YOU CURIOUS YET?

"NASONI"

3
PANTHEON

4
ST. IGNATIUS OF LOYOLA

• Nasoni Hunting

Are you feeling a bit thirsty as you walk around Rome? Don't worry, there are 2,500 *nasoni* in the city!

Yes, you heard me correctly. Nasoni (which means "big noses" in Italian) are drinking FOUNTAINS. They were named nasoni because the shape of the spout resembles a big nose!

• Would You Like a Suppli?

And what if you're feeling a bit hungry? That happens to me a lot!

THEN TRY A SUPPLÌ!

It's a kind of elongated croquette filled with rice and a meaty tomato sauce. Hidden inside is a small piece of *mozzarella* cheese.

CASTEL SANT'ANGELO

Raise your shields my valiant friends; a castle awaits us!

Originally, despite its name, there weren't any knights at Castel Sant'Angelo, because this imposing building was actually a large TOMB intended for the emperor and his family! HADRIAN had it built in 123 AD, almost two thousand years ago! It looked very different back then: it was a circular mausoleum made of volcanic tuff blocks, all covered in white MARBLE. Over the centuries it underwent many transformations: a castle, a luxurious refuge, and even a court with a prison!

• A Secret Passage

Around 1300 AD, Castel Sant'Angelo became an impenetrable fortress, complete with ramparts and moats, where the Pope could hide out if he was in danger. They even built A SECRET PASSAGE, which is an elevated walkway, between the Papal Palace in Vatican City and Castel Sant'Angelo.

LET'S GO UP TO THE TOP SO YOU CAN SEE IT BETTER!

• The Legend of the Archangel

In 590 BC, Rome was struck by the plague. According to an old legend, one day the Archangel Gabriel appeared on top of the structure, in the act of placing a bloody sword in its scabbard, thereby announcing the end of the epidemic. A statue of the Archangel was placed on top of Hadrian's Mausoleum in gratitude.

NOW CAN YOU GUESS HOW THE CASTLE GOT ITS NAME?

PIAZZA NAVONA

Welcome to Piazza *"in agone"*!

No, I haven't mixed up the name! In ancient Rome, that was what this square was called. In Latin, *agones* means races or games, and in fact back then the square was a STADIUM, where athletes could compete in front of 30,000 spectators!
Later *"agone"* became *"navone,"* and eventually *Navona*!

• A Lake in Piazza Navona

In 1652, POPE INNOCENT X inaugurated a very curious custom: in the summer, when it was very hot, the spouts on the three fountains were left open, thereby allowing the water to flow into the square.
Piazza Navona then became a small LAKE that citizens not only used to cool off, but also to have lots of fun: there were wooden and papier-mâché boats, gondola-shaped carriages, and musicians who played standing in the water!

Seek and Find

- 5 paper boats
- 1 coachman with a wig
- 3 ducks
- 3 frogs
- 1 lady in a red dress.

• The Fountain of the Four Rivers

In the center of the square, there's the stunning Fountain of the Four Rivers, which are personified in four huge statues. The monument was designed by the famous sculptor GIAN LORENZO BERNINI.

What rivers are they? Well, the giant figure surrounded by prickly pears represents the *Rio de la Plata* in South America. The one with his eyes covered is the *Nile*. The statue holding the oar is the *Ganges*. And the fourth one is the *Danube*.

THE PANTHEON

Follow me, friends! We're standing before
one of the world's largest ancient buildings!

The *Pantheon*, built by the Roman general and architect MARCUS AGRIPPA, was a temple dedicated to all the gods. The giant dome, which is still one of the biggest in the world, was added a century and a half after it was built! The building's only window, which is a large oculus (a sort of "eye") with a diameter of about 30 feet (9 m), is in the center of the DOME. Legend has it that it was once closed with a large bronze pine cone, but when the temple was donated to Pope Boniface VI, who transformed it into a church, evil spirits removed it so they could escape!

• How Old is the Pantheon?

To find out, we have to look for the Latin inscription under the tympanum:

"M-AGRIPPA-L-F-COS-TERTIUM-FECIT," which translates as "Marcus Agrippa, son of Lucius, built this when he was consul for the third time." Knowing that Agrippa's third consulate dates back to 27 BC, we can say that the Pantheon was built between 27 and 25 BC.

• What if it Rains?

According to legend, it doesn't rain inside the Pantheon.

There is actually some truth to this due to the "chimney effect." The hole creates an updraft, which helps to turn drops of light rain into vapor.

But, if the rain gets heavier, there's nothing to stop it, and it's collected in holes in the floor.

SAINT IGNATIUS OF LOYOLA

Are you ready to go into one of the most "magical" churches in Rome?

On one side of the charming *Piazza di Sant'Ignazio* is the facade of a beautiful Baroque church. The original plan included the construction of a large dome, but it was never actually built. But somehow, when you go inside, there is indeed a dome! So, HOW IS THAT POSSIBLE?

• Mystery Solved

The dome you see if you stand on the floor marker near the altar is nothing more than an OPTICAL ILLUSION! A "trick" created in 1685 by the artist ANDREA POZZO, who painted the frescoes using a special technique that makes the painting appear three-dimensional, and therefore real.

You'll discover another optical illusion if you go and stand on the gold disc in the center of the nave, and look up: a church overlaps the real one, but WITH THE SKY INSTEAD OF A ROOF!

THE CAT ON PALAZZO GRAZIOLI

Keep your eyes open, kids, we have to look for a cat!

On top of the cornice on Palazzo Grazioli, there's a statue of a small cat, which the street is named after. The statue was once part of the decorations of the ancient temple of Isis.

BUT WHY IS THE STATUE OF A CAT TO BEGIN WITH, AND WHY WAS IT PUT ALL THE WAY UP THERE?

• Meowww

According to an old legend, one night a cat that lived in the neighborhood saved the inhabitants from a fire by alerting them with its loud meows.

Another legend says it saved a child: a little boy was leaning out of the window and was about to fall off the sill, but the cat warned the child's mother, who arrived just in time to save him.

NO ONE KNOWS WHICH OF THE TWO STORIES IS TRUE, BUT EVERYONE AGREES THAT THE ANIMAL IS LOOKING AT THE HIDING PLACE OF TREASURE. TOO BAD NO ONE HAS EVER ACTUALLY FOUND IT!

VATICAN CITY

Vatican City is the smallest country in the world!

And to think that its surface area isn't even 0.2 square miles (0.5 sq. km), which is equal to about 60 soccer fields. Like all independent states, the Vatican mints its own coins (although its currency is still the euro), has its own stamps, and is protected by the smallest army in the world. The Head of State is the Pope, who is also the religious leader of the Catholic Church.

The Vatican, which is surrounded by medieval walls, is on the edge of Rome's old city center, and most of it is occupied by *St. Peter's Basilica* and its immense square. There are a few other buildings, one of which houses the extraordinary *Vatican Museums*.

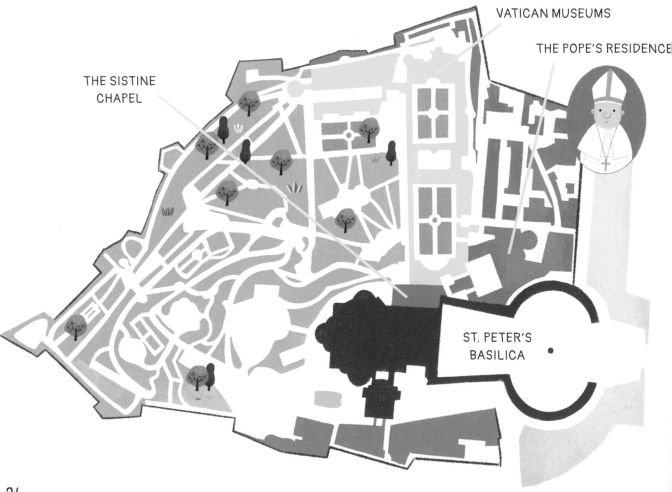

VATICAN MUSEUMS

THE POPE'S RESIDENCE

THE SISTINE CHAPEL

ST. PETER'S BASILICA

• The Vatican Museums

The Vatican Museums are home to one of the largest and most important art collections in the world. The best way to visit them is to rent an audio guide for children, which offers a fascinating tour, including a map and even a treasure hunt that involves finding works of art.

Accompanied by music and engaging, fun explanations, you'll discover paintings, sculptures, galleries full of maps, and even mummies and sarcophagi!

YOU'LL ALSO FIND THE STATUE OF LAOCOÖN IN THE MUSEUM: IS THAT A SNAKE WRAPPED AROUND HIM?

• The Pope's Small Army

The Pontifical Swiss Guard is made up of 110 men who protect the Pope night and day, accompany him on trips, and watch over the city. They are easily recognizable due to their striking uniform: blue, red, and yellow stripes, with puff sleeves and puff pants. They also carry two cold weapons: a sword and a halberd!

ONE OF THE MOST EXTRAORDINARY ARTISTIC MASTERPIECES IN THE WORLD CAN BE FOUND IN THIS SMALL COUNTRY.

TURN THE PAGE IF YOU'RE CURIOUS TO FIND OUT WHICH ONE IT IS!

THE SISTINE CHAPEL

The *Sistine Chapel* is one of the world's greatest artistic and cultural treasures. It was built in the 15th century, at the behest of POPE SIXTUS IV.

In 1508, the Pope asked MICHELANGELO to fresco the huge ceiling, the surface of which is 5,382 square feet (500 sq. m): A TRULY TITANIC JOB!

• Look Up
One of the first problems that MICHELANGELO encountered was how to reach the 65-foot (20 m) high ceiling. The artist designed a simple wooden platform that rested on supports anchored near the windows, leaving the space below free, yet at the same time making it impossible to see his work. Michelangelo painted standing up, looking up at the ceiling, non-stop for FOUR YEARS. It's said that he was so absorbed in his work that he didn't even go home to sleep! This caused him severe muscle aches, dizziness, and problems with his eyesight.

• I'll Do Everything Myself
Michelangelo was only commissioned to paint the TWELVE APOSTLES, but when he finished, he'd painted over THREE HUNDRED figures! The extraordinary artist illustrated the entire history of humanity before the Ten Commandments: the Creation of Adam, the story of Noah, the Book of Genesis, and the Old Testament. It's said he didn't trust anyone, and that he painted almost the entire ceiling by himself!

Follow me, kids, another part of Rome awaits us!

1 JANICULUM HILL

TIBER

2 MOUTH OF TRUTH

ITINERARY 3

Today's itinerary is full of unusual and mysterious places: we'll start from the *eighth hill of Rome*, where we'll witness an EXPLOSIVE event at noon! From here, we'll walk down into the *Ripa neighborhood*, where a strange bearded character will ask us for our hand! Then we'll look for a snake on a ship-shaped island, after which we'll climb another hill; a magnificent place dotted with bitter orange trees, where there's is a keyhole we just have to peek through.

3
TIBER ISLAND

4
AVENTINE HILL

• Pasquinades

Once upon a time, there were six "talking" statues in Rome. Well, they didn't really talk! During the night, people would hang cards on them, with poems, or sarcastic phrases criticizing the rulers, or pointing out the city's problems. These "pasquinades" were named after PASQUINO, the statue upon which today's Romans still attach witty, satirical messages today.

• The Tiber

Rome is crossed by the Tiber, the third longest river in Italy. It was once called the *Albula*, from the Latin *albus*, which means "white," or light, in reference to the color of the water. According to an ancient legend, it owes its current name to *Tiberinus*, a strict river god who one day fell into the river and DROWNED.

JANICULUM HILL

Come on, let's get moving. We have to make it up the hill before noon!

Rome's eighth hill is close to *Vatican City*. From up here, you can take in a magnificent view of the metropolis below.
And every day at noon, a cannon is fired.
BOOM!
Don't worry, kids! It's perfectly safe!

• Infallible Clock

It's said that a long time ago, in 1847, POPE PIUS IX was annoyed by the fact that the midday bells never rang at the same time.

To solve this problem, he ordered a CANNON to be fired every day at exactly 12 o'clock...

...SO THAT THE BELL-RINGERS WOULDN'T HAVE ANY MORE EXCUSES!

• A Lighthouse Far From the Sea

On the beautiful walk up the *Janiculum Hill*, there's even a lighthouse. But what's a sentry of the sea doing here, if there's no sea?

Actually, this splendid monument has nothing to do with sailing.

It was a gift from a committee of Italians living in Argentina.

On special occasions, the lantern projects the colors of the Italian flag onto the city's rooftops.

CAN YOU TELL ME WHAT THEY ARE?

Seek and Find
- 1 child eating a maritozzo pastry
- 1 girl eating a suppli
- 1 man eating pizza
- 2 cats
- 1 balloon.

MOUTH OF TRUTH

Who's that weird, bearded character?

It's a large, round slab of marble depicting a face, set in the wall of the portico of the *Church of Santa Maria in Cosmedin*. The eyes, nostrils, and mouth are all hollowed out.

No one really knows whose face it is. Some say it's JUPITER, others the sea god OCEANUS, and some even think it's a FAUN. What we do know is that there are some sinister mysteries behind this strange mask.

• A Lie Detector

Originally it was a manhole that "swallowed" rainwater, but from the Middle Ages onwards, there were numerous legends about it: the most widespread of these claimed that the mouth had the gift of ascertaining the truth.

DO YOU KNOW HOW?

The accused had to put their hand in the opening: if they were telling the truth, their hand would come out unscathed; if not, the mouth would close and their hand would be cut off!

WOULD YOU LIKE TO TRY? ARE YOU BRAVE ENOUGH TO PUT YOUR HAND IN ITS MOUTH?

TIBER ISLAND

*In the middle of the Tiber, one of the smallest
inhabited islands in the world!*

It's 984 feet (300 m) long and 98 feet (30 m) wide, and is connected to
both sides of the river by two BRIDGES. It's said that it was once shaped like
a ship, with a bow, a stern, and a "mast" in the middle!

• Asclepius's Snake

According to an ancient legend, when Rome was struck by the plague over
two thousand years ago, the Romans sent a ship to Greece so they could
pray to the God of Medicine. When they reached their destination, a large
snake came out of the temple and took refuge on the ship. Believing it to
be Asclepius himself, the men took it back to Rome, where the reptile threw
itself into the river and swam to Tiber Island. It then disappeared, along
with the plague!
A TEMPLE WAS BUILT ON THE ISLAND IN HONOR OF THE GOD, THE RUINS
OF WHICH CAN STILL BE SEEN TODAY, ALONG
WITH THE FIGURE OF A SNAKE!

IF YOU LIKE MYTHS
ABOUT ANCIENT ROME,
THEN TURN THE PAGE!

EVERY STATUE, EVERY MONUMENT, AND ALMOST EVERY STONE IN ROME HIDES A STORY, A LEGEND, OR A MYTH

DO YOU KNOW WHAT MYTHS ARE? They are stories recounting the deeds of gods, demigods, or even monsters, such as GIANTS.
They were written to explain certain events, to answer certain questions, or to celebrate feelings of strength, courage, hatred, or love.
I'M GOING TO TELL YOU TWO OF THEM.

• Hercules and the Monster of the Aventine Hill

It's said that somewhere on the *Aventine Hill*, there was a cave inhabited by the terrible giant CACUS, a fire-breathing creature with yellow teeth, whose body was covered with hair. One day, HERCULES, the demigod with extraordinary strength, arrived in Rome with a herd of beautiful red cows he'd stolen from the giant GERYON. Tired, he fell asleep near the Tiber, but upon his awakening he discovered that some of the cows had disappeared. CACUS HAD STOLEN THEM. Hercules went into the giant's stinking cave covered with bones, and killed him with his club.

THE NEWS SPREAD, AND TO CELEBRATE THE HERO, THE PEOPLE BUILT AN ALTAR IN HIS HONOR.

• Aeneas and the Founding of Rome

The ancient city of Troy was besieged by the GREEKS, who used a brilliant strategy to burn it down. Some soldiers hid inside a huge WOODEN HORSE, which the Trojans had brought inside the city walls, believing it was a gift for the gods. But when night fell, the Greeks dropped out of the big wooden animal and destroyed the city while everyone was asleep. That same night, a fearless hero named AENEAS dreamed of his friend HECTOR announcing the defeat, urging him to set out to found a new city. And so he did. After countless adventures, Aeneas reached Italy and got married. Do you know who two of his descendants were?

ROMULUS AND REMUS! TURN TO PAGE 47 TO LEARN MORE!

AVENTINE HILL

What an amazing view, and the air up here is so fresh and clean!

The Aventine is one of the seven legendary hills upon which Rome was built in ancient times. It's a magical place, where you can stroll among roses and orange trees, like those in the beautiful garden that overlooks the city. But it's also a place full of mysteries, legends, and unexpected surprises. My favorite time to come up here is at sunset, because you can see Rome bathed in red and orange light. Ahh-woo! Forgive me, my friends, but I'm a very romantic wolf!

• Spying Allowed!

In *Piazza dei Cavalieri di Malta*, right on top of the hill, there is one of the few places in the world where you can peep through a keyhole without looking like you're spying on someone.

WALK UP TO THE LARGE DOOR OF THE VILLA DEL PRIORATO, AND PEEK THROUGH THE KEYHOLE: THE SPLENDID DOME OF SAINT PETER'S WILL APPEAR!

• A Miraculous Plant

The keyhole at the *Villa del Priorato* isn't the only space worth peeping through. Inside the nearby church of *Santa Sabina*, there's a small crack in the wall of the CONVENT GARDEN, through which you can see the oldest *bitter orange tree* in Europe.

Legend has it that it was brought here from Spain by *Saint Dominic* more than 800 years ago, and since then it has continued to grow, bearing fragrant flowers and beautiful fruit every year.

37

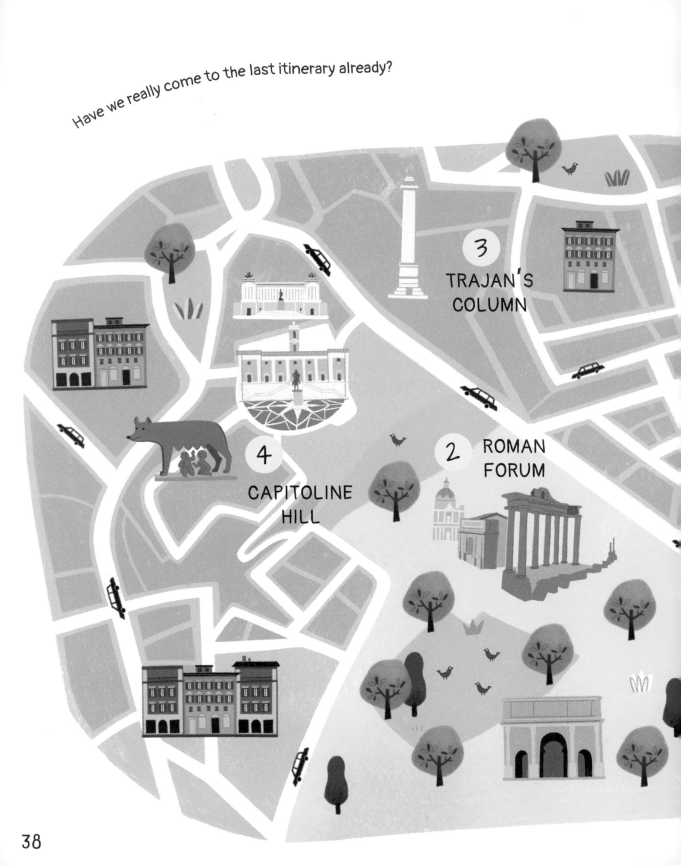

Have we really come to the last itinerary already?

3 TRAJAN'S COLUMN

4 CAPITOLINE HILL

2 ROMAN FORUM

ITINERARY 4

Our last adventure starts in one of the most famous places in the world: a huge *amphitheater* where brave GLADIATORS once fought. After hearing some stories and fun facts about it, we'll go to the impressive ruins of the *Roman Forum*, where we'll pretend to be archaeologists and learn about a mysterious legend.

We'll try to read the stories on *Trajan's Column* as if they were comics, and finally we'll climb the LEGENDARY *CAPITOLINE HILL*, on which there's a museum with a very special statue.

BUT FIRST, SHOULD WE HAVE BREAKFAST?

MARITOZZI

1

COLOSSEUM

• A Sweet Hiding Place
A *maritozzo* is a typical Roman pastry with ancient origins. It's a soft, sweet bun, stuffed with loads of whipped cream. Yummy! Legend has it that young men hid engagement rings inside them, and then offered them to their girlfriends. If they said yes to the marriage proposal, they'd become "maritozzi," which means husbands!

• The Numbers on Via Trionfale
There's a street in Rome with very special numbering. For a long time, the street numbers weren't in the traditional order, but instead indicated the distance from *Capitoline Hill*. The last number is 14,159.

CAN YOU IMAGINE LIVING IN SUCH A HOUSE?

THE COLOSSEUM

Welcome to the largest Roman amphitheater in the world!

Roman Emperor VESPASIAN ordered the *Colosseum* to be built between 70 and 72 AD, almost 2,000 years ago! To celebrate its completion, his son TITUS, who had succeeded his father, inaugurated the amphitheater with *one hundred days of games*. The gigantic arena had, in fact, been built to offer citizens a place for entertainment. Thousands of spectators could watch shows, re-enactments, fights, and even real naval battles!

• The Horrible *Venationes*

In the morning, shows with ANIMALS were held in the Colosseum. Titus had them sent from all over the empire: ostriches, lions, crocodiles, bears, camels, and many other exotic species, which appeared in front of the audience as if by magic, pulled up into the arena in invisible "elevators."

Sadly, they were often cruel games: fights and combat in which both men and animals lost their lives.

• Gladiator Fights

Gladiators fought in the afternoon. They were usually slaves, criminals, prisoners of war, or men who'd been sentenced to death, who had been trained rigorously.

THE BATTLES TOOK PLACE IN THE ARENA, A WOODEN PLATFORM COVERED IN SAND, WITH TRAP DOORS AND HOISTS CONNECTED TO THE UNDERGROUND TUNNELS, USED TO MAKE THE BATTLES MORE "SPECTACULAR."

Seek and Find

- 1 retiarius (gladiator with a trident and net)
- 1 murmillo (gladiator with a sword and rectangular shield)
- 2 fierce beasts, also hidden among the spectators.

FIND OUT MORE ABOUT THE COLOSSEUM!

• Why is it Called the Colosseum?

Originally it was called the *Flavian Amphitheater*, but in the Middle Ages everyone began calling it the *Colosseum*. In Latin, *colosseum* means colossal, GIGANTIC, and, given the huge size of the monument, it's easy to see why they chose this nickname.

According to other sources, however, the adjective referred to a huge statue of NERO that was close to the arena.

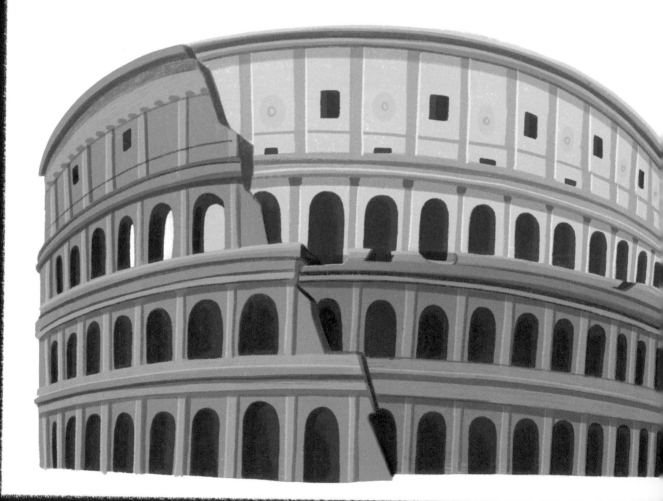

• *Naumachiae*: Naval Battles in Ancient Rome

It seems that the *Colosseum* was equipped with a special mechanism that could fill the arena with WATER. The amphitheater therefore became a "sea" on which thousands of prisoners fought each other aboard biremes, triremes, and quadriremes, which are types of ancient boats!

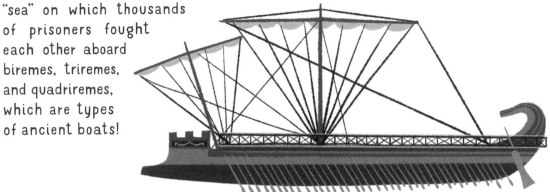

• The *Velarium*

When the weather was bad, or on hot, sunny days, expert sailors from an offshoot of the Roman fleet would COVER the amphitheater with a sort of awning. When it was especially hot, jets of SCENTED WATER were sprayed on the spectators to, um...combat bad smells.

• Thumbs up, Thumbs Down

In many modern gladiator films, the emperor decides to save the defeated fighter by turning his thumb up. If, on the other hand, he decides to condemn them to death, he turns his thumb down.

Actually, it seems that this isn't how it worked in ancient Rome: a thumbs up symbolized a drawn sword that kills, while a clenched fist indicated the sword being put back in the scabbard.

PRACTICALLY THE OPPOSITE!

THE ROMAN FORUM

Follow me, kids, let's walk up to the panoramic point
overlooking the forum!

Every column, stone, and ruin that you see in the Roman
Forum was once a temple, a church, an arch, or a palace. It
was the heart of Rome's political and social life; a large "town
square" in which purchases and business deals were made,
important meetings and events were held, and where people
prayed.

TRY TO IMAGINE WHAT IT WAS LIKE!

• The Legend of the *Lapis Niger*
Just over a century ago, an archaeologist made an extraordinary discovery:
hidden under some dark marble slabs near the *Curia*, he found an important
sacred area. And here, on the base of an altar, was a stone block with the oldest
Latin inscription ever found.

It said: HE WHO DAMAGES OR VIOLATES THIS PLACE SHALL BE CURSED!

Legend has it that the tomb of *Romulus* was located
here. Who was Romulus? Find out on page 47!

TRAJAN'S COLUMN

It's time to go to the Imperial Fora!

As Rome expanded, one forum was no longer enough, and over five more "squares" were built. These were called the Imperial Fora (that's the plural of forum!). In Trajan's Forum, the last and largest of them all, there's a huge and fascinating monument; a column that's one hundred Roman feet high, which is more or less the same as 6 GIRAFFES PLACED ON TOP OF EACH OTHER!

• Ancient Comics

The most extraordinary thing about it is that the entire column is carved with incredible stories, which recount Emperor TRAJAN'S conquest of DACIA.
It looks a bit like there's a paper scroll wrapped around it, which has to be "read" like a comic book.

USE BINOCULARS TO SEE THE CARVINGS AT THE TOP!

CAPITOLINE HILL

The *Capitoline* is the smallest of the seven hills upon which Rome was built. It was once home to the city's most important temples, and thanks to its elevated position, it was a strategic place for defending the city. There's a steep cliff here called the Tarpeian Rock, and according to one of the many legends about it, TARPEIA, a young woman who betrayed the Romans by letting the enemies into the fortress, was thrown over the edge. Hence its name, and also why it became the place where people condemned to death met their fate, thrown off the cliff!

• Geese Guards

You should know that the GAULS besieged Rome over two thousand years ago. Local citizens took refuge on the hill, but one night the enemies found them.

IT WAS ONLY THANKS TO THE HONKING GEESE THAT THE ROMANS REALIZED WHAT WAS HAPPENING, AND MANAGED TO SAVE THEMSELVES!

• Capitoline Museums

Piazza del Campidoglio is home to the oldest public museum in the world! The most fun way to visit it is with the audio guide for children, which recounts FASCINATING STORIES about the statues on display. Before saying goodbye, I want to tell you one of my favorites...

Many centuries ago, the land that would one day become Rome was ruled by a cruel man called Amulius. He had the twins Romulus and Remus thrown into the Tiber, knowing that they would be entitled to the throne. Fortunately, the current carried them to shore, and the children were saved by a she-wolf who nursed them.

ROMULUS BECAME THE FOUNDER OF ROME. AND WITHOUT MY ANCIENT ANCESTOR...WELL, MAYBE THIS MAGNIFICENT CITY WOULDN'T EVEN EXIST!

THIS IS WHERE OUR JOURNEY ENDS! GOODBYE, MY FRIENDS!

LAURA RE

Laura Re was born in Rome, where she attended the Roman School of Comics. She then started working with animation studios as a character designer, concept artist, and illustrator. After attending the International School of Illustration in Sàrmede, she moved to Milan to get a master's degree in illustration. There she furthered her knowledge of publishing and the world of children's illustrations.

DANIELA CELLI

Daniela Celli was born in Florence in 1977. After studying piano at the Luigi Cherubini conservatory, she moved to New York, where she began studying criminology. In 1997, she returned to Italy and got a law degree, as well as a diploma from the Academy of Dramatic Arts. She has always been passionate about travel, and in 2008 she began writing a blog about her adventures around the world with her family.

Graphic layout: Valentina Figus

White Star Kids™ is a trademark of White Star s.r.l.

© 2023 White Star s.r.l.
Piazzale Luigi Cadorna, 6
20123 Milan, Italy
www.whitestar.it

Translation: TperTradurre s.r.l., Rome, Italy
Editing: Katherine Kirby

First printing, September 2023

ISBN 978-88-544-2011-3
1 2 3 4 5 6   27 26 25 24 23

Printed and manufactured in Poland by Ozgraf - Olsztynskie Zaklady Grafic

FSC® MIX
Paper from responsible sources
FSC® C178000

One of Lupetta's ancestors was none other than the famous she-wolf who suckled Romulus and Remus.
Lupetta absolutely loves singing, she adores sunsets and maritozzi with whipped cream, and she knows the hidden secrets of every single stone in Rome!

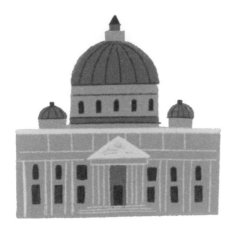